Deal Me In

Deal me in, when you're playin'
that game called love
Deal me in, when you're playin'
that game called love
Deal me in to that mortal sin,
love is blind, but I don't mind
Deal me in when you're playin'
that game called love.

> As sung by Marvin Dykhuis
> Author unknown

Jesse Taylor virtually re-invents the meaning of music and harmony every time he places his fingers on the strings. The past few years have seen him turn his attention to drawing ... drawing which is as colourful, dynamic and shape shifting as his music. These illustrations are the perfect complement to Alyce's poetry.

This book rocks like a 45rpm on Wes McGhee's jukebox and whispers love songs in the same breath. Alyce McCullough Guynn ... a Texas girl who became a writer and never forgot how awesome *'Party Doll'* by Buddy Knox was. I love her and you will too.

> --Terry Clarke, writer/musician. Recorded albums include *Call Up a Hurricane, Lucky, Sound of the Moon, Green Voodoo,* and *Rhythm Oil.*

Earthy, electrically visceral and unfailingly honest, Alyce Guynn's sharp observations hit you like a song you didn't know you needed to hear until the moment it starts playing on the radio. You don't have to "get" poetry -- whatever that means -- to get what Guynn's driving at; a working appreciation of life will do.

> --Patrick Beach, AUSTIN AMERICAN STATESMAN, author of *A Good Forest for Dying*.

With words that are as steeped in wisdom as they are wonderfully strung together, Alyce Guynn makes her mark in Texas' distaff literati. Call them naïve or folk art, Jesse Taylor's illustrations give Guynn's *Deal Me In* a memorable, hard black edge.

> --Margaret Moser, AUSTIN CHRONICLE.

DEAL ME IN is full of risky, funny, heartbreaking laments that are never sentimental, always honest, and devoid of self-pity. Alyce Guynn writes, "I am unwilling to walk out before the final act." Like a card player with a hard-earned reputation, she plays each hand for what it's worth. These are not poems about winning or losing. They are about "conveying us closer to the self we are seeking."

> --Hayan Charara, author of *The Alchemist's Diary* and *The Sadness of Others*.

Poems
by
Alyce Guynn

Illustrations
by
Jesse Taylor

2005

Pearson Publishing Company
Corpus Christi

Copyright © 2005 by Alyce M. Guynn.

All rights reserved. No part of this book may be reproduced or transmitted in any form or by any means, electronic or mechanical, including photocopy, recording, or any information storage and retrieval system, without prior written permission from the publisher, except by a reviewer who may quote brief passages in a review.

Library of Congress Control Number: 2005931180

ISBN-13: 978-0-9768083-0-5
ISBN-10: 0-9768083-0-7

Photograph on page 146 courtesy of Terry Tammadge.

Photographs of author and artist on cover and on pages 151 and 155 courtesy of Butch Hancock.

Cover art: Playing Cards by Jesse Taylor, front cover
The Ace of Roses by Jesse Taylor, back cover

Cover design: Katherine Pearson Jagoe Massey
Book design: Katherine Pearson Jagoe Massey
with suggestions from Alyce Guynn and Tamara Schleman.

Published by
Pearson Publishing Company
Corpus Christi, Texas
www.PearsonPub.US

This book is dedicated to the memory
of
Mary Alice Davis
who loved words and had quite a way with them.

Patience, and shuffle the cards.

—Gini Coleman

The Full Deck

Wildcards
"Deal Me In" song quotation, page iii
Dedication, page vii
In Gratitude, page xiii
For Alyce McCullough Guynn by Terry Clarke, page xv
Poet's Perspective, page xix
Artist's View, page xxi

The Shuffle

One:	Allison's Theme, page 3
Two:	Inviting Love, page 5
Three:	Angels Are Wild, page 7
Four:	Caddie's Song For Michael, page 9
Five:	Willow Road, page 15
Six:	Wheel Of Love, page 19
Seven:	I Found My Jazz, page 21
Eight:	Alpha, page 25
Nine:	Better Than I Can, page 27
Ten:	Beside Still Waters, page 29
Eleven:	Black Leather, page 31
Twelve:	Surrender, page 33
Thirteen:	What I Like About Men, page 35
Fourteen:	Reflections, page 37
Fifteen:	Mother Of Mercy, page 41
Sixteen:	Blue Wind, Big River, page 43
Seventeen:	Kiss Farewell, page 47
Eighteen:	Cherish The Rose, page 49
Nineteen:	Mary Pearl, page 53
Twenty:	Never Time To Say Good-bye, page 55
Twenty-one:	Water On Rock, page 61
Twenty-two:	Stir Carefully Through The Days, page 63

Twenty-three:	Living In The Mists, page 65
Twenty-four:	Surfacing For Words, page 68
Twenty-five:	Coming To The Bone Man, page 71
Twenty-six:	Still Life, page 75
Twenty-seven:	An Open Hand, page 77
Twenty-eight:	Sailor's Last Leave, page 79
Twenty-nine:	Tattoo, page 83
Thirty:	This Boat Called Longing, page 87
Thirty-one:	Letting Our Teenagers Loose, page 89
Thirty-two:	Destined, page 93
Thirty-three:	Scarlet Ribbons, page 95
Thirty-four:	Jazz Valentine, page 97
Thirty-five:	Crow's Flight, page 101
Thirty-six:	Freight Train To Forever, page 103
Thirty-seven:	Touched By A Grievous Angel, page 105
Thirty-eight:	Traveling Memories, page 107
Thirty-nine:	Assuming The Radiance, page 109
Forty:	Refrain Of Yearning, page 111
Forty-one:	Roller Coaster, Carousel, page 113
Forty-two:	God On Our Block, page 115
Forty-three:	Unfaded Love, page 117
Forty-four:	Red Moon On Water, page 119
Forty-five:	Kisses, page 121
Forty-six:	Under The Yellow Moon, page 125
Forty-seven:	Once In A Blue Moon, page 127
Forty-eight:	Love Or Something Like It, page 129
Forty-nine:	Denouement, page 135
Fifty:	Last Waltz, page 139
Fifty-one:	Revisiting The Cards, page 143
Fifty-two:	Jesse's Song, page 145

Jokers

Ace of Roses, page 147
Citations, page 149

Alyce Guynn
Biography, page 151
Bibliography and Awards, page 153

Jesse Taylor
Biography, page 157
Art Catalog, page 159
Discography, page 161

In Gratitude

My heart-felt gratitude goes to those who have encouraged my writing and/or mid-wived this book. I have received a lot of support on this journey, from many sources, in a myriad of forms – from financial help and hands-on editing to healing hands and prayerful hearts. It is my earnest hope that I remember to mention everyone who deserves thanks, but if I forget, please forgive. In gratitude, I name:

Kippy Jagoe Massey, Rudie Berger, Jim Davis and Jan Demetri, Mandy Mercier, Alice Embree and Carlos Lowry, Bobby Nelson, Lori Hansel, Char Dethloff, Allison Trosclair, Adrienne Evans, Butch Hancock, Terry Clarke, Marvin Dykhuis, Dana Burton, Peggy Lynch, Susan Bright, the women of High Moon Writers, Cheryl and Patrick Fries, Pat Marshal, Terry Tammadge, my colleagues in the Antitrust Division, Anya Rylander-Jones, Lisa Soileau, Beth Moose, M.B.S, M.M., Brighid, Bran, Faol, and Eala, Allison Smith, and, as always, my children Geoffrey, Justin and Mercy for sharing their mother with her Muse.

And, of course, Jesse.

For Alyce McCullough Guynn

As I recall, I first met Alyce Guynn in Austin, Texas on the evening of Saint Patrick's Day 1994 where I was performing at a special concert hosted by Jimmie Dale Gilmore for the occasion. We were introduced to each other backstage and she invited me to a dinner party at her house the following week. We already shared many mutual friends and some of those were at that initial shindig too, including 'Slim', my accordion playing friend from London who played on *'Rhythm Oil - The Sessions'* the album I cut with Michael Messer and Jesse 'Guitar' Taylor. Jesse was also there.

I mention these things because music and the love of it runs through both of our lives and friendship like a river.

Alyce read her poem *'Caddie's Song for Michael'* that night. With it's image of a girl 'humming an Everly Brothers tune'. It captivated me ... she read a lot of others too ... I sang a lot of songs as well. The dinner party over, people drifted away and a handful of us stayed, sipping whiskey while I sang through the night. I fell asleep for about an hour at dawn and finally bid adieu at dusk the following evening. I don't know why but I have a vivid memory of singing Jesse Winchester's *'Yankee Lady'* out on the lawn with Alyce's beloved West Highland terrier Elvis scampering around as evening fell.

In her poem 'Allison's Theme' she says

'If I'd had a lick o' sense
I'd have married Donnie Gililland
when I was 19' .....

Maybe she should have but she wouldn't be the Alyce I know and love would she?!

We were both born October babies and draw inspiration from the autumn, it's misty mystique and blazing colour. One of my favourite pieces of her writing is *'Pumpkin and Cinnamon on Parade'*. Alyce graciously has given me permission to use it for the booklet of my (as yet unreleased) live album *'A Night in Baton Rouge'* ...

The colors of autumn summon us to inquiry
Overriding the summer's blindingly bright hues
With subdued shades of russet and ochre
The wine reds of winter are hinting at the corner
As pumpkin and cinnamon stage their brief parade
Before conceding to cranberry, bayberry, holly and pine

This season is mine, above all others
October's child running wild among fallen leaves ...

Dawn and dusk has arrived and departed many times since that first evening in 1994 and many things have changed in both of our lives since then but our friendship has remained a constant.

We share many precious memories of hours spent in the public arena and in the company of dear friends, some of them now departed; Champ Hood, Glen Alyn. I mention them now because I know they would be excited about this publication too but then I'm pretty sure they had a bearing on it's direction anyway.

This edition is especially noteworthy because it also features the drawings of Jesse 'Guitar' Taylor, as well as a photographs by Butch Hancock. They both tore out of Lubbock with Joe Ely to illuminate our lives with their songs and guitar playing. Guitar playing ? ... Jesse Taylor virtually re-invents the meaning of music and harmony every time he places his fingers on the strings. The past few years have seen him turn his attention to drawing ... drawing which is as colourful, dynamic and shape shifting as his music. These illustrations are the perfect complement to Alyce's poetry. Here Jesse and Alyce have teamed up to create a work as forceful as a speeding freight train and as romantic as a country-side carousel.

This book rocks like a 45rpm on Wes McGhee's jukebox and whispers love songs in the same breath.

Alyce McCullough Guynn ... a Texas girl who became a woman, became a mother, became a writer and never forgot how awesome *'Party Doll'* by Buddy Knox was.

I love her and you will too.

Terry Clarke
Carmarthenshire, Wales.
September 2005

Terry Clarke is an Anglo/Irish writer and singer who was born in Berkshire in the Thames Valley west of London, England. Four of his ten albums were cut in Austin, Texas, the first *'Call Up a Hurricane'* in 1988. Since then he's been a regular visitor and regards it as his second home. In 2001 Clarke moved to Argyll in the west of Scotland and has recently re-located to west Wales, near Swansea the birthplace of Dylan Thomas whose writing first inspired him to work with words.

www.terryclarke.com

Poet's Perspective

The writing of these poems spans more than a decade; the subject matter encompasses most of my life. Inspiration has come from loves, losses and yearnings over the years. When I wrote "Caddie's Song for Michael" more than 12 years ago, I was still more enamored with yearning for something out of reach than I was ready to receive what was being offered. Since then I've learned how to say *yes* whole-heartedly, and some of my poetry reflects those changes. However, the part of my Celtic soul that hears a sea song, retains its propensity for yearning, and will always surface in my writing.

The book has been a series of fortuitous chances and convergences that felt like miracles. What began as an urging from Peggy Lynch, a well-loved Austin poet who has offered me countless encouragement and opportunities, to compose a simple chapbook, soon transformed into a publishing offer from Pearson Publishing Company. What started out with me seeking permission from my close friend Jesse Taylor to use his "Playing Cards" on the front cover, turned into a full-scale collaboration and partnership, the result of which is this book full of art as well as words. This partnership with Jesse has been one of the most energizing and creative experiences I've known.

To have our mutual long-time friend Butch Hancock shoot the cover photo added a special touch, bringing the project full circle. Butch and Jesse have traveled the planet playing together and have known each other since youth. Butch's lyrics have inspired me for more than three decades, and his music soothed my soul. He has been present for several of my major life events, including the wedding of my oldest child, the birth of my youngest, so it seemed more than fitting that he have a hand in this book. Add the brush stroke of Terry Clarke's written introduction, and *Deal Me In* became a convergence, not only of creative effort, but community. Like Butch, Terry is a long-time mutual friend to both Jesse and me. He has traveled, performed and recorded with Jesse and has inspired and encouraged my poetry from the beginning. His Irish roots and my Scottish lineage found immediate common ground in the Celtic Ray.

Motherhood and writing have been two major identities all my life, writing pre-dating parenting. I saw my first poem published at the age of twelve, and I was pregnant with my first-born when I was nineteen. This project has exhibited similar qualities to procreation, from its spring-time conception, its quickening in the summer, the winter labor and delivery – a full nine-month gestation. Surrounded by loving, supportive friends, I'd say it's been more like the intimacy of home birth, rather than the clinical hospital environment. Now that we've got this baby here, I hope to watch it grow healthy and strong.

Alyce Guynn
Austin, Texas
October 2005

Artist's View

I met Alyce Guynn in about 1988, as she was good friends with many of my musician compadres. I got to know her through the many gigs I played with various singer-songwriters that she would come to.

We became close friends. In March of 2005, Alyce was working on a book of her poetry and asked me if I would give her permission to use my drawing "Playing Cards" for the front cover. She sort of had a theme that dealt with playing cards. Then she asked me if I would draw a special playing card for her to use at the end of each poem in the book. I thought yeah, why not, it would be fun.

I did the illustration "Ace of Roses" for her, but as I began to read through the poems, other images started to come into my head. The deeper I got into the poems, the more I wanted to illustrate some of them. Alyce was all for that.

This began a series of illustrations that I became obsessed with. Whereas I originally intended to do nine or ten, I wound up doing thirty. This has been a great learning experience for me, seeing as how I'm used to doing larger colored illustrations and was confined to black (charcoal pencil) and white on a much smaller area.

I have thoroughly enjoyed this project and hope you enjoy it as well. This is great stuff from Alyce and I sincerely appreciate this opportunity to be a part of it. Enjoy!

Jesse 'Guitar' Taylor
Austin, Texas
October 2005

Deal Me In

Allison's Theme

If I'd had a lick o' sense
I'd have married
Donnie Gililland
when I was 19.

He worried that he was too white
(Johnny Winter not the only dynamite
Albino Texas guitar player),
but in truth,
he probably revered me more
than I could take at the time.

I rejected his marriage offer
but was moved
to trembling, tumbling tears
by his musical tribute
Allison's Theme
debuted before
a thousand jazz fans;
Maynard Ferguson
in the wings.

My subconscious
musta tried to correct
my immature mistake
for I've spent the rest of my life
falling in love
with guitar men,

Continued

even though in marriage I chose
a bassist, then a fiddle player
neither of whom revered me
like Donnie did.

Now, this wise woman I have become
has a wee bit of insight
into why I do the things I do.

But in matters of the heart
I remain a little girl.

Turning away
when I should say *yes*
then yearning
for what might have been.

Inviting Love

If love lingers at your door
awaiting an invitation to come in,
greet her with extended arms,
usher her to the most comfortable chair,
offer a cup of tea.

Let not love remain a stranger
but befriend her;
court her with enticing songs
and fragrant scents
from far off lands.

Keep fresh cut flowers
at hand, ready to bestow
upon her.

Let her get to know you.

For when love lives
in the home of your heart,
you need not go a looking.

Angels Are Wild

Here's the game:
angels are wild
hearts are trump
and there's no way
to finesse the queen.

Count your points
the hand is dealt
play for keeps.

It's win for the maiden
win for the jack
no jokerman
no Diamond Jill.

Just a draw
from the deck
and the thrill
of the call.

Caddie's Song For Michael

Caddie'd been up all night
at the Janis Christ Café,
eyes all red, fingers puffy,
and those little wrinkles 'round her mouth
running deeper than the South Fork
of the Little Red right after a hard rain.

She was humming an Everly Brothers' tune,
swaying in and out with a gaze that could see
straight through steel.

She slipped up on me quietly,
with the intent of a spider,
circling me with the dark of her eyes,
embracing me in the light of her seeing.

Those long painted nails, nectar,
tapped on the table
beckoning, I think, some unseen safety net
so she could free fall into the space
created by the all nighter at the café.

I don't go there any more,
but I can remember the cavern
of emptiness looming like dawn about to break
the first available heart.

She wore the ruby ring,
the one Michael gave her
when she was twenty-seven, fresh and trusting.

Dancing rubies, circling shadows.
Caddie leaped off
into the bounding black of night
leaning in on me, wild of heart, eager for truth.

Here is what she told me:

> *I have known love, both sipped it sweetly*
> *and spat it bitter from my lips.*
>
> *I have embraced love like a lion's roar,*
> *hugged it tight, licked it like candy,*
> *swirled it loose like silken scarves.*
>
> *I have known love, the kind that eats you,*
> *the kind that drips from your pores,*
> *the kind that aches inside your thighs*
> *like a slow-moving train.*
>
> *I have known love like starlit summer nights*
> *with lightning bugs in flight and peaches*
> *hanging*
> *heavy on the branches, falling ripe.*
> *Dogs chase crazy while little girl blue*
> *lies on her back near the fig bush,*
> *dreaming on the stars, drifting.*
>
> *I have known love like lightning*
> *streaking through the sky,*
> *crackling currents burning in its mission,*
> *leaving a slow sizzle after the fire glowing.*

Continued

*I have known love like touch of new skin
soft against a rainbow, evening shade,
kisses the grass, morning dew
meets my lips, begging.*

*I have known love drowning
deep in ocean wave,
violent storms come rocking, bloody sea
waters too dark for swimming.*

*I have known love like bullets shooting
splitting hide, shouting.
I have known love like waterfall
in crystal springs shining
where poems are plucked from trees,
fruit grows ripe in summer.*

*I have known love holding hands
with teddy bears and Ferris wheels,
seeing the gypsy lady.*

I have known love bleeding.

I have gnawed the bones of love dying.

*I have known love flying on bird's wing
like white dove singing.*

*I have known love angels bring
in the quiet, still of morning when dusty sky
hovers at the edge of night waiting.*

Continued

*I have known love that walks the hallways,
lockers banging, heavy leather jacket
weighted.
I have known love of long nights
sitting by the window,
staring into the sky, hoping.*

*I have known love near death, teasing
until the heartbeat dies in the pillow talking.*

*I have known these loves and more,
yet, none remains so pristine as that one
never tested,
the love who lives in memory,
dancing in my shadow,
the love on the hill, yearning.
No promises made, no promises broken.*

That said, Caddie stilled her voice.

We both knew she spoke of Michael.

As her dark eyes settled,
she reached her hand to touch me;
my skin burned.

And I saw a halo of light
circle the curls of her hair.

Willow Road

While you were riding the rails, gambling life,
I caught carrousels in fairy tales
where young damsels needed rescue.

When you warmed from winter's cold
by a hobo fire, listening to the wolf cry,
I bathed naked in the sparkling waters
of wonderment and awe,
petting a baby fawn.

A miracle that we chanced to meet
and make love amongst the stars.

Yours, an urgent burning;
mine, an ancient yearning,
reaching for the rain.

We walked the willow road
swaddled in the silence of those
who have traveled the journey
more than time out of mind.

It was the quiet that kept us,
the road that called us,
the wolf and fawn trailing behind.

Continued

There among the rushes,
where the river widened and ran wild,
you lay me down an innocent child,
and taught me to mend.

The only sin was,
I made you my god.

Wheel of Love

We grew up in cotton fields,
called each other by nicknames.
We loved then like cousins
telling secrets.

You teased and pulled my pigtails,
later convincing me to play in ways
more forbidden.

We were family. *Familia*

Then, when we found each other
in a different time and space,
we embraced our past as though
we'd never stepped out of overalls
and red bandanas.

My little girl still deferred to you,
grown tall and worldly;
you remembered the forbidden
with which we'd played,
rekindled it. *Amor*

This love we bathed in,
let it wash over us without regret.

The longing held us; we were happy
just to know.
Then, as time grew short,
the yearning deepened,

Continued

tempting us with cupid's cup,
where we supped on bittersweet nectar,
nibbling at each other,
never asking questions
or retracing mistaken turns. *Eros*

As the wheel turned
we rode into the familiar,
returning to the fertile soil
where we'd first planted our affection.

Content in the comfort
that fate had restrained us
from leaping
into what could have destroyed
one or both of us
and eaten away
at the unconditional nature
of our love.

You kiss my eyes.

We hold the other in kindest regard,
kneeling in common prayer. *Agape*

I Found My Jazz

I found my jazz.

I thought I'd lost it,
but, no, it was just

hidden away.

First time I found it,
I was young.
It was summer
and I carried a scent
of gardenia in my walk,
a hint on bare shoulders,
and it drove my young man wild.

Jazz nights.

Scotch and soda,
big bands,
small combos.

Pizza and beer jazz.

I married a jazzman,
had a jazz baby;
trombones and trumpets.

Jazz to the bone.

Blue lights,
blue notes.
The basics:
Miles and Maynard,
Elliot and Pound.

Jazz, Mama, jazz.

I found my jazz
and I'm singing it,
swinging it all around me
like burning incense
in a procession.

I found my jazz
and I'm digging it
like it was something
new and undiscovered,
like baby wrinkles,
like little hands
in beach sand.

I can dig it.

My jazz came back.
Hallelujah do waw de bah.

Betting on the bay,
strutting fancy,
winking.

I found my jazz.

Finally, after all this,
and it is still hot,
it is still cool.

It's what I've got.

Jazz, Mama, jazz.

Alpha

This white bull roams among his herd
not raging, but gazing afar.

His testicles swing in rhythm
with his prance,
exposing a rose tattoo;
silken ribbons adorn his horns
like the knight wearing
his lady's token into battle.

He takes his time, not threatening
nor even asserting dominion,
yet ramping up, getting ready
to make his mark.

When at last he has seen enough,
allowed enough grazing and gazing,
he rises up, his power billowing
in clouds of dust.

He claims his mate, takes her.

She surrenders.
No protest, no hesitation.

Continued

No denying the obvious
nor crying out
against his reign.

Then he snorts, paws the ground,
rallies the rest into the fold,
holding all attention
between his eyes.

King bull.

Better Than I Can

We never lied or tried to hide
our feelings;
even though we both
did our share of retreating.

Knowing now what I do,
I see that day I walked away,
no explanation.

One among many.
Strong is my propensity
to abandon.

But God or Grace
gave us the gift of return
and you grabbed me,
would not let me go
before we took time to say
what had been left unsaid,
to put in play our yearnings,

To live for the moment
where love abounds.

You know me better
than I can.

Beside Still Waters

If I were tossing the coins
they would say
after sorrow comes joy.

If I were listening
to Butch Hancock, he'd sing
*a rose cannot bloom
the whole year long*
and question my ability
to stand slow spells.

If I were spreading the cards
the eight of swords
would be my self,
the two of cups, hope and fear.

Here in this lonesome valley,
I am wishing to lie down
beside still waters
and reach for the rod and staff
of comfort.

I am waiting
for the waning moon
so I can watch it
grow full again.

Black Leather
for Bobby

When I was a teen I'd climb
into your old Pontiac
and we'd go park;
I was more than willin'.

You were older, divorced,
had served some time;
I was in high school,
wild, unwillin' to be tamed.

One day my daddy
came at you with a co-cola bottle
threatening to kill you
if ever you came 'round me again.
He'd caught me skipping school
to be with you. *It was only a P.E. class;
after all, I was a straight-A girl.*

He succeeded in driving you away;
but only drove me deeper
into my desire for black leather
and slicked-back hair.

Continued

I still love to take the dare
prefer a working man's simple honesty
over educated innuendoes
and games of hide and seek.

Even now black leather and long hair
catch my eye, quicken my breath.
And I still like to go for a ride,
make out in the car.

Surrender

Under the canopy of ancient oaks
and glittering lights,
I listened to fortune's call.

Fate reached over, tapped me on my shoulder.
I acquiesced without regret.
Surrender comes
easier with age.

A neon halo encircled us
as I raised my eyes
to the heavens in praise.
Grace granted us another chance,
and this time I did not run away
or constrict in fear.

I let you lay me down
before the fire and whisper.

I let you love me.

You give me sacred secrets
to hold safe within my heart;
I give you my trust, long withheld
from all the others.

We sleep sweetly inside the sphere;
allow our dreams,
awake renewed.

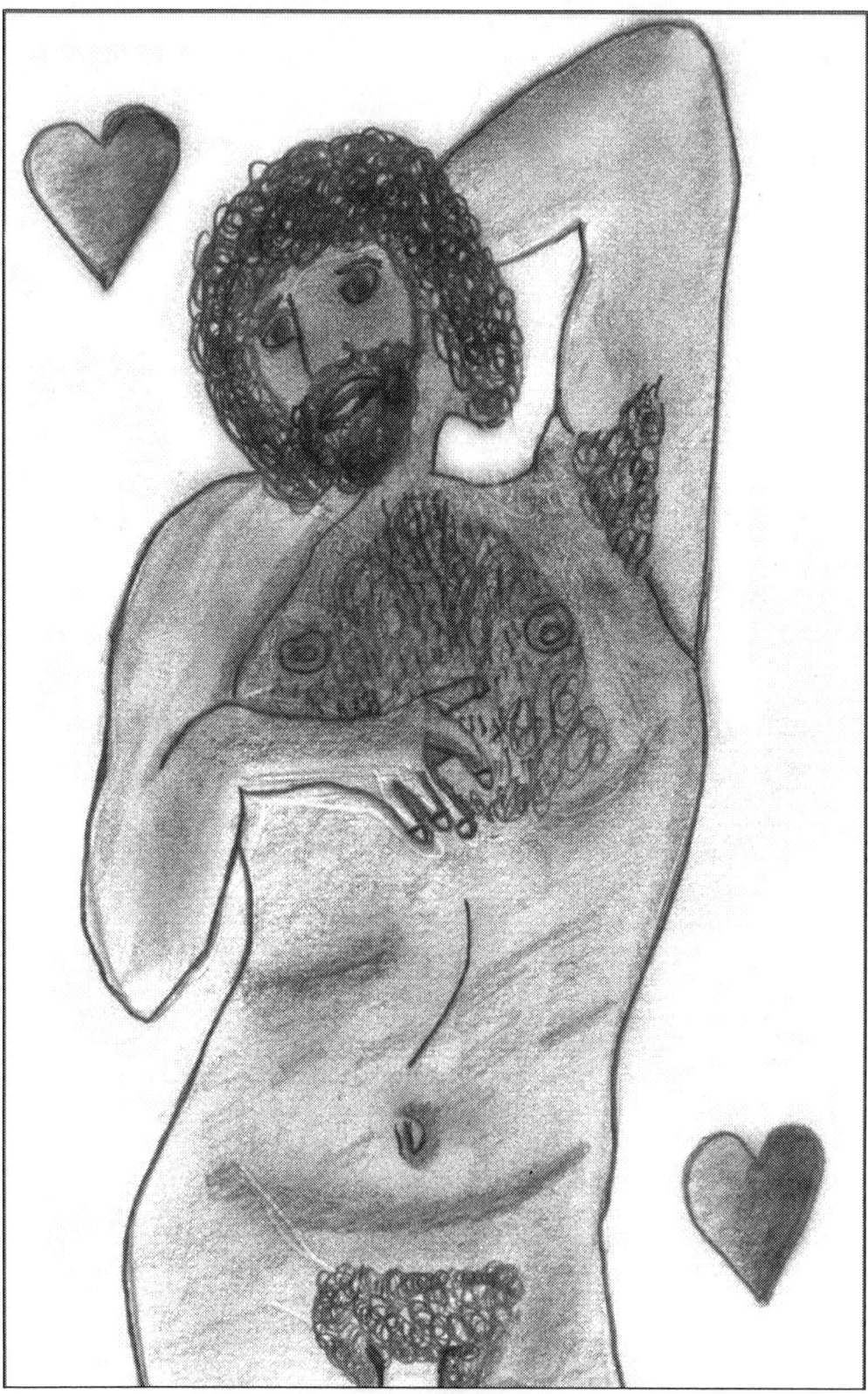

What I Like About Men

These are the things I like about men:

First, and foremost, they are other
so very much of what
I'm not.

I love their fur,
their dangle.

I like to feel their heat
rising, know their
cool, calm acceptance.

I like the lank of long legs
slung out in repose.

I like the sweet sweat
of their exuberance.

The men I like the most
do not need to suit up
except when absolutely necessary
but rather,
meet the world relaxed, as is,
in the comfort
of self confidence.

Continued

I like the romp and stomp
of a man
experiencing excitement. I like their
hard bodies and soft hearts.

I like it when
they beat the drum,
strum the strings.

I like it when
they ride wild horses,
chasing dreams.

I like it when
they sail the seas, and
when they fish the streams.

I like them most
when they love
admire and
honor me.

Reflections

Like the ancient Celts
who refused to duplicate
an exact image of any
living creature,

I distort the picture I paint of you,
not from disrespect,
but from some still and holy
reverence of who you are.

As I behold in awe the
essence of your being,
I am blinded by your light,
relying only on second sight
to see beyond the mist of time
enfolding us.

The gifts you bear to me
glitter as golden as the crowns of kings.
I am blessed, then blessed again
each time you cast your eyes
to see me standing
in wait of some distant tolling.

Continued

You listen mindfully to my song;
you ken my meaning.

When I bend my knee
to look into the river,
it is your reflection
I see.

Queen of Heaven

Mother Of Mercy

In our happy days,
when these trials
were only foreshadowed in song,
we liked to shuffle the deck,
lay the cards upon the table.

Tell me, I said,
which witch you think I am--
Queen of Hearts or Spades?

You took your time,
then giving me your
most wicked grin, said:
Neither, my dear,
you are the Mother of Mercy,
Queen of Heaven. Now succor me.

I am recalling our playfulness
with affection,
trying to laugh my way
through this vale of tears.

Blue Wind, Big River

Somewhere between rumor and sigh
I got lost in the coyote's call,
stumbling into your shadow
but a watchful angel broke my fall.

The night the blue wind
wrapped her hungry arms around us,
you crawled inside my skin
seeking comfort.

I let you
relish my secrets.

We waded into the cold marshes
where you tasted my shiver;
your eyes held promises
of escape across shallow waters.

Leaning against your resolve,
I let you lead me through
the mystery
of no destination.

And there, among the blackbirds
and the thrushes,
the sun set inside us.

I was willing to swim
in your sorrow.

But I refuse
to drown
in your blood.

Kiss Farewell

It was the days
of rabbit fires and wars
when we lived
among the roses.

Women veiled our faces
and wore silken skirts
that rustled when we walked.
Men were gallant, eager for quests,
thirsty for battle.
They loved the ladies, but
rarely took them.

The cards fell before us,
royals holding court,
as we read them for signs,
played them with circumspection.

Somewhere in our castle
a knight knelt before his lady,
knowing his impending journey
will lead to darkness and uncharted land.

We held hands at dusk
risking it all in the garden
where the dew fell fresh on the roses.

Continued

Your whispered words
echoed through the wind,
etched the sand.

There, in the silence of starlight,
you lifted my veil,
pressed your lips to mine,
bidding me a fond farewell
before mounting the black stallion,
leaving me, to seek the grail.

No promise
of return.

Cherish The Rose

I cherish this bruise,
arising not from anger or abuse,
but from eagerness.
A winter rose blooming
on a dreary day.

I like the little hurt you left me,
so when I touch myself and it stings,
I feel you, remember your taste.

Your scent, all over me
marking me, making me yours;
I don't want to wash that away.

I want to hover in the air
above our bed and be led
over and over into the magic.

Soon the bruise will fade;
the little hurt lose its sting.
I can't go without bathing
so I have memorized your breath
upon my breast,
your fingertips tracing my scars,
your face at peace beside me.

Continued

I tuck tiny parcels of our love
in hidden corners
and deep pockets of memory
so I can retrieve them, relive them
when you are away.

Mary Pearl

I keep a picture of Our Lady
next to my own personal
high priestess. One wears
a golden halo; the other is
encircled by a furry, white hat.

One exposes her Sacred Heart;
the other offers up another piece
of hers.

Come on, come on, come on.

One is modestly cloaked in soothing blue;
the other, bedecked and bejeweled,
sporting feathers and velvet.

One smiles serenely,
conveying comfort
that is yours for the asking;
the other grins mischievously,
hinting at what is yours
for the taking.

You know you got it, if it makes you feel good.

Both are my icons. The Madonna
and the good time girl,
both a part of me.

Continued

One reaches down to cradle me;
the other, calls me
to give it all I can.

Come on, come on, come on.

Never Time To Say Good-Bye

> *Lightning never takes a long time*
> *It's just a flash across the sky*
> *Hardly time to say 'how are you'*
> *Never time to say 'good-bye'*

"Lightning Never Takes a Long Time"
by Al Grierson

I wear this ring to remind me
of your devotion.
You gave it on a whim,
this plain gold band
that to the world
symbolizes some legal arrangement
between man and woman.
But for you,
it was simply a token of affection,
a touchstone for me to hold near,
when you were away.

I touch it often, offering up little prayers
for your safe return into the arms of one
who will cradle you against uncertainties
as you journey into the unknown.

Continued

I've been retracing our steps,
reviewing precious moments,
so as to renew, as well as preserve.
No mistake when I call your name,
an intentional affirmation of "no separation".

At times this reviving
brings me comfort;
others, tears.

I am doing the best I can. Allowing fears
to float to the surface
where I face them,
avoiding the undertow.

Remember the time
we drove all night
to New Orleans?
You held my hand all the way
across the Pontchartrain.

We rented a musty room
in the Evangeline,
where we shed all constraints and obligations
dogging our daily lives.
We holed up
in the room all afternoon,
playing poker,
waging small intimate pleasures.
Slow dancing to Aaron Neville songs,
stumbling onto the street just before dawn,
leaning on you,
your laughter
taking my weight.

Continued

Then there was Mexico
where you spoke French
to the waitress.
We were stripped searched
on the way back, at the border.
You sang to the cab driver
that Warren Zevon song
about being on the outskirts of town.
We slid inside the murals,
pretending angel wings.

And all that walking
in the rain.

Remember when
you borrowed that Harley
for a ride along the coast?
We tossed our helmets
into the ocean to feel lighter.
We were so free then.
You were at last unshackled
and I, pardoned for all my past mistakes.
We took to the wind,
ending up on a communal farm
where you hid me
from my vigilante ghosts.

That time beside the lake,
the band played our song
and you took me aside on the grass,
tickled me 'til I nearly wet myself.
We lingered late and tipped generously
because we'd been such tough customers--
you, sampling all the import beers and
I, persnickety about the food temperature.

Continued

Once you called from Dublin
wanting to toast the New Year.
I ran for the Jameson's
and we raised our glasses
over the phone,
across the waters,
vowing never to forget.

Oh, these memories
come tumbling down around me,
bubbling up from the abyss of then and now,
until I am submerged in you.

You had all those years, well-wishers
attempt to console, not knowing

It was just a flash across the sky.

Water On Rock

It wouldn't have worked
had you rushed me.

I needed time to take it all in,
wanted spaces in between,
to let the moonlight settle on my skin.

You came with a gentle confidence.
Wouldn't let me walk away.
Courted me in stages, remaining calm
even when I became a skittish colt
ready to bolt out the door.

This, in part, because you know me,
but also because it is your way
never to press or push
but stay persistent.

Water on rock,
you wore away my resistance.

Now I am yours.

Stir Carefully Through The Days

I've been rummaging
around in the past,
digging up memories,
retrieving the tape recording
where you sang
into my answering machine.

Savoring old photos
where we sat cheek to cheek
in a booth sipping whiskey
and spinning funny stories.

Remembering all the reasons
why I love you.

Wanting more.

Living In The Mists

I wear black silk for you,
you who elevated appreciation
of underwear to a fine art.

Tonight I smear St. Andre brie
on bread, instead of breast,
nibbling it off toast,
no substitute
for your firmness.

I douse myself with rose oil,
minding cleavage,
and crevices you
admired, explored
with enthusiasm.

You are crossing to safety,
leaving me behind
in the dangerous delicacies
of memory.

You said if I'd let you,
you'd love me eternally.
I do.

Continued

You swore forever and ever
and sealed it with gold.
I won't remove it.

You asked me to light your way.
I will.

Here in the dimness of candle
I retreat to nestle with you,
near as my heartbeat,
true as my breath.

A golden glow envelopes us,
enshrining our pledge
fulfilling the promise.

I will not forget.

You found your way
into my very essence;
there you will live forever.

It is here I abide,
asking not for more,
but awash in amazement
that fortune granted us so much.

Many live a lifetime
with a great deal less.

We have been blessed,
kissed by the kiln
where passion is fused with trust.

We are among the lucky
who taste the wafer
of unconditional love,
drink the holy wine
of uncommon communion.

And while I release
that part of you who must go,
I cling to the piece
who mingled with my soul,
merged in the mystic,
timeless mists of time.

I will let you
love me
eternally.

Surfacing For Words

It was the day
of the Wolf Mother;
we trailed behind
awaiting the witch doctor
to bring his bones
with which to bless us.

You, with your soft
swaddling voice and silver hair,
me, so tongue-tied,
coming up for air
from months of suffocating redundancy,
afraid to utter one word
lest I be repeating.

Now we have no need to ponder the question
nor to quest for gold.
The story has been told
in eleven languages
under the sun
and the departed rejoice
in its telling.

We no longer tarry,
but quicken our feet to follow,
for the Mother leaves no field
fallow for long.

Continued

Soon we will pluck sweet fruit
and slide it between our teeth
to tease the lost memory
of when I
was reticent
and you
were full of words.

Coming To The Bone Man

I am kneeling bare before the bone man,
wearing black crow feathers in my hair,
face painted blue,
begging him to take my fears,
make me ready for your love.

Bone man reaches in his rattle bag,
blessing me with smoke,
healing me by fire.

I dance naked to the moon,
stepping in and out of her shadow.
The white horse waiting for my ride.

I raise my arms in praise;
our lady has sent me someone to love.

Now I ready myself for you,
releasing old loves,
outworn ideas, new fears, bloody tears
and send them in flight into the night.

Bone man reaches across the flame,
names me.
I take his hand, invoke the smoke.

We dance, the bone man and I.

He shakes his gourd, I toss my mane,
forsake all others,
I prepare for you.

Continued

The bone man chants his magic song.
I sing along in a foreign tongue.
He reaches into his rattle bag,
presents me with a sacred stone.

The bone man dances around me,
dusting me with ashes from the fire.

Blesses my black crow feathers,
my enchanted stone.

I am walking through the fire
to face your love.

> I will not come to you unholy
> full of fear.
> I welcome you as the king stag,
> come to you a high priestess,
> leave a goddess.
> We will create our own universe
> under the sheltering sky.

I cry out to the bone man
to burn away yesterday's betrayals,
cleanse me in the holy smoke,
pour for me the water of life.
He puts the cup to my lips.
I stand before the bone man,
reaching out my hand to take the drink.
I beseech him to make me ready
to receive your love.

Continued

I am dancing in dark shadows, turning
toward the fire burning, dancing in circles,
swaying to the night music, the moon's majesty.
He sifts the ashes, sprinkles my head.

My wolfhound howls
at the stillness of the night,
lifts her head skyward, finds the moon full.

I dance with the bone man,
entranced, smoke rising.
He rattles his bones, beats the drum,
chants his ancient song
and I fall down on the ground,
pounding my hands against bare thighs.
I call out your name.

I name you tonight
at the holy fire.
I rub ashes on my skin.

Cleansed of my fears,
I claim your love.

I have come at the midnight hour;
I have come in fervent prayer.

The crow flies across the sky,
a shadow on the moon; I swoon.

The fire is hot, the wind, wild.

Continued

I dance for you,
chant my ancient song.

Sacred wound, healed by fire.
I expose my heart
to share secrets of my soul.

The bone man blesses me, declares me
smoke-cleansed, holy water washed,
ready to receive your love.

He wraps his bones
and bird fathers,
his stones and potions,
closes his rattle bag and
drifts into the distance.

I sit by the embers and ashes.
I hear your song
coming through the night.

I await your love.

Still Life

A faded photograph,
frayed at its edges,
slightly out of focus,
shows me
wearing a tattered rabbit skin coat
purchased at the Purple Heart for seven dollars.
It swings mid-thigh,
falling open
for lack of buttons.
The lining, though torn,
was softest silk.

That day my hair,
brushed with boar's bristles,
smelled of rosemary oil.
It shines in a waterfall of waves,
unstructured, natural curls,
cascading down my back.
Yours tumbles over your coat collar,
wild and unruly,
like your eyes.

The camera catches you clowning,
as you bend your knee
in mock plea for forgiveness,
or entreaty to partake
in some wacky scheme.
Your lanky legs are folded
into flea market jeans,
shabby with patches sewn on the knees.

Continued

Your boots are scuffed,
the left heel slightly worn down.
Your smile spreads a thin beard
across your cheeks and chin.

We are on the wharf,
waiting for a ship to come in.
The photographer has captured
our carefree abandon,

Our attitude of *forever young*.

I keep the picture,
a study in black and white simplicity,
juxtaposed to my still life with roses.

The still life displays colorful flowers
spilling from a crystal vase
into a round bowl,
full of bright red strawberries and cherries,
where they remain forever fresh.

Just as our youth is
frozen and framed.

An Open Hand

It was a time of turquoise and abalone,
scarlet ribbons and silver shoes;
a time of tequila sunsets
with soft mandolins.

You, with your motorcycle boots
and shiny black hair,
making much of the journey;
I, with tangled intentions
and divided loyalties,
aiming at perfection.

Our sun-filled days and endless nights
wove a fragile web
where we hid our love away,
searching each other
until we discovered self.

We watched with dismay
as the snow bird flew
managing to repeatedly
kindle our fire,
until the warmth we sought
no longer satisfied.

And our need for the sweetly familiar
gave way to desire for freedom.

Continued

You rode off one autumn day,
leaving me neither withered
nor weeping.

In those days we invited change,
welcoming an emptiness,
waiting to become
full.

Sailor's Last Leave

In a companionable quiet,
bred of intimacy and affection,
we walked at water's edge,
our eyes cast down
in search of shells,
our hearts lifted up
by crisp, clean air
and the undeclared trust
that settled between us.

You were on leave.
Our time was brief,
mandating we live every moment
fully, which we did,
utterly aware of the uncertainty
and possible calamity,
threatening our future.

Those moments coalesced
into a lifetime of memory,
preserved and framed;
a picture drawn in pastels,
where muted sunlight

Continued

dances across the waves
and seals laze on large rocks,
singing our sea song.

The painting hangs
on the wall of my heart.

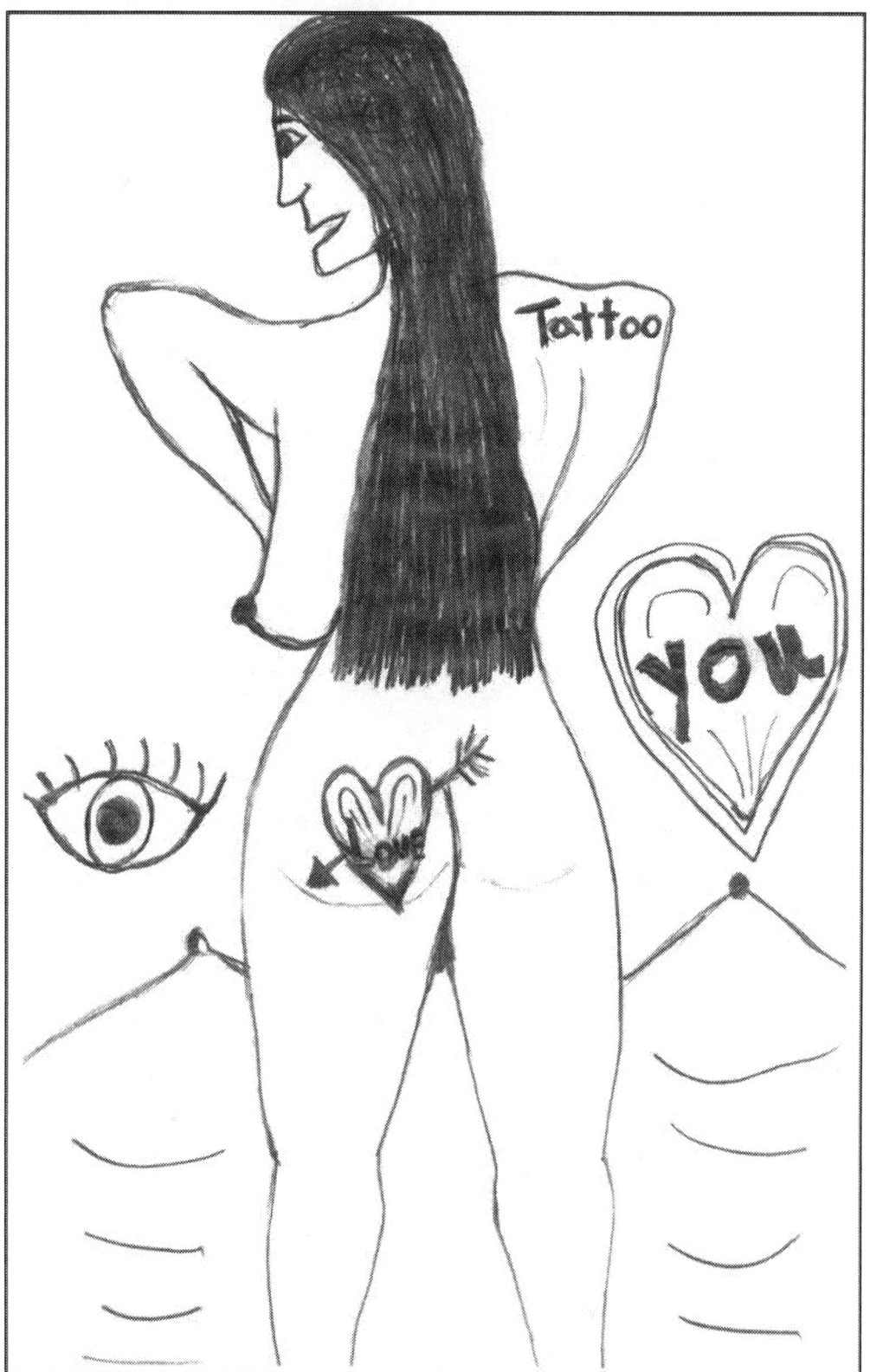

Tattoo

You teased me
about getting a tattoo
on my bottom.

What I didn't tell you was
I already had your name
tattooed on my heart.

It's been there
a long, long time.

Maybe since we were kids
chasing lightening bugs
and rolling down grassy slopes,
tumbling onto each other,
laughter cradling the collapse.

We had our hopes up,
dreaming of distant islands,
wishing ourselves into
some Mediterranean warmth
as the Blue Norther rattled our teeth
and your certainty took my breath.

Always you believed in me,
never plunging into doubts
that swallowed me whole at night,
dried my bones to brittle in daylight.

Continued

Our love sustained me,
even when your absence
settled inside me, a cavernous void
cawing like the wily raven.

Now you keep a lock of hair;
and I wear the ring --
reminders when we are apart.

Your name,
tattooed on my heart.

This Boat Called Longing

She made the sign of the rose;
he made the sign of the cross
as they boarded their boat
to navigate this wide river.

Kneeling in the bow,
he blessed the vessel
while she chanted
sea songs
free of secrets.

This boat that carried two,
christened "Longing,"
seemed so small
for such a journey.

They created comfort between them
a quiet quilt, void of fear,
where they nestled,
awaiting the waning moon.

She did not disappoint them,
attaching herself
to the darkest part of sky
to shine through the mist.

Continued

Thus they traversed
the river, out to sea
where neither friends nor foes
rose in greeting.

Only vast water,
a welcoming womb,
eager to receive them.

This Longing
ferrying them home.

Letting Our Teenagers Loose

When we were teens
you'd remove my bra (34-B),
fool around with my titties.
Then you'd go down,
I'd call out your name.

Now we're grown older and wider
(my cup now D), yet we like
to let our adolescents out to play.
Making out at stop lights,
messing around in parking lots,
displaying public fondling.

You still drive me wild
and I can make you smile
at the most unexpected moment.

But you are gentler now
and I, more trusting.
We've been blown by the wind,
tossed upon unsettled waters
enough times to know
nothing is certain
and everything changes.

Continued

So we relish the chance more,
delight in delicious samplings.

I still call your name.

Destined

She's the kind
of woman
who would
wear the moon
in her hair and
breathe stars.

Her belly, full
of beautiful butterflies
whom she birthed
one at a time
to form the earth
beneath her feet
the sky above and
the ocean deep,
where she dove
to meditate
her own madness.

He's the kind of man
who would
devour his lovers
raw or half cooked
over an open flame
of forgiveness.

He liked to hunt affinities,
divulge identities
and master the crooked dog

Continued

who lifted his leg
in fiendish defiance.

He wore his rage
in pelts draped
across his chest;
his crown cut sores
and left scars
on his head.

They met perchance
one day,
bathing in the river.

She swooned;
he saved her.

They lived happily
ever after.

Scarlet Ribbons

Like a prayer for
scarlet ribbons
answered in
pre-dawn mystery,

Some unseen,
unnamed spirit
placed on my pillow
scent of your skin.

An unclaimed memory
emerging from deep waters
drowning in neglect.

Jazz Valentine

I'm riding with Paul Ray.

He's playing Deano crooning
in his sultry divulgence,
I'm Confessing That I Love You;
Nancy Wilson imploring
Someone to Watch Over Me.

Thank goodness someone
with a little love perspective
requests *Alfie* by McCoy Tyner.

What *is it* all about?

Then there we are
in a smoky bar;
you whisper something
to the piano player
as you step down
from the stage.

You glide to my table,
pulling me from my chair
as your band launches into
Try a Little Tenderness.

You are tall,
swarming with music,
easy in your skin.

Continued

I am wearing black satin,
slick under the palm
of your hand.

You rest it just below
my waist
pressing me
across the dance floor.

We glow in the dark.

You were the one
who knew how women
do get weary.

You were the one
who sent roses,
poured 18-year-old Scotch,
sang my favorite songs.

You gave me
jazz valentines.

Now I listen
to the radio,
remembering.

The set ends with
The First Time Ever I Saw Your Face.
And my heart trembles
*like a captive bird
that is there at your command.*

Crow's Flight

A bell, a chime, a turning wheel
a shadow lost, a wish at will.
The time has come, the moment gone.
We danced all night, went home at dawn

It's been a long, long time
since the belonging.

Your ghost appeared, your face was near.
You crooned the words "I love you."
The moon hung high, the tide was low.
You had a sad song upon you.

It's been a long, long time
since the belonging.

The sky seems coy; the air blows free.
The black bird flies away from me.
Her wings in flight tell secrets of the ocean.
Your song, steeped in emotion

It's been a long, long time
since the belonging.

Freight Train To Forever

The freight train
is approaching, coming in
on dragon's wings;
it's fiery breath
fueling for a heavy load.

We wait by the tracks
pitching pennies,
taking bets on
who will first hear its whine
or see the smoke.

It's roar, rumbling toward us,
echoes thunder in the midnight sky;
when lightning flashes,
iron sparks fly.

The plaintive howl, now near
as the dessert coyote,
interrupts our play,
reminding us of choices,
chance and circumstance.

Without words,
we rise in expectation,
discerning no more
than an impending storm.

Continued

And, when, as if
by some act of God,
the engine slows,
in unison we hop aboard,
ready for the ride
that will carry us
to no known end.

You gather me close,
repeating your vow,
forever, and ever,
as we allow
the road to unfold.

Touched By A Grievous Angel
for G.P.

I am not God or the Goddess
not even Morgan or Merlin
but, if the power were mine,
I would slip into green silks
and silver shoes to glide
across the great divide
and pluck you from the wheel
where you were crushed by fate.

I never sang high lonesome harmonies
to your honeysuckle melody,
nor did I lift the veil to meet your eyes,
raise my lips to receive your kiss.

Yet, I sensed such a familiar knowing
from other worlds
where once we lived,
and would gladly walk all the way
from clean mountain stream
to warm gulf waters
to see you whole,
to hear you sing again.

Whether in the humid
voux doux, Crescent City
or arid desert sands,
bury your bones
or send you away
in ceremonial flame.

Continued

I had no say.

You, too young to die,
left your handprint upon us
listening to the music.

I go months leaving you among
the memories of those days
when I was in alive in romance,
slow dancing down all those roads,
quoting your verse in love letters.

Then by chance,
I hear you from the past,
come calling through the air.
I listen to your laughter
scattered here and there
and anew, you touch my heart
in some unimaginable
inarticulate place
where abides
melancholy of lost dreams
wasted laments, yearnings.

You, like no other,
reaches the part of me
who opens to love.

Your voice behind
my song of longing.

Traveling Memories

Your memory is a nomad
traversing my life.

At times, it camps
outside my city gate
where at night
I feel your presence,
but do not invite
you to dine or sup.

Others, your scent is far away,
washed in some distant river
where the fish are unfamiliar
their colors, unrecognizable.

Then there are the times
when you walk through my door
bringing gifts from foreign shores,
singing a new song
you learned on the road.

I remain receptive.

Assuming The Radiance

I never thought to ask
where the rose got
her radiance,

always
assuming it was
in the blood.

I never thought to question
where you found
your song,

always
assuming it was
on the road.

I never thought to wonder
where the sun
got its splendor,

always
assuming it was
spun from gold.

I never thought to doubt
that you loved
with all your heart,

Continued

always
assuming the truth was
in your eyes.

In the blood,
on the road,
spun from gold,
in your eyes –

There it lies.

Refrain Of Yearning

Softly in summer rain.
I hear the refrain of our yearning.

It spills onto the grass
in grace notes of intimacy.

It contains each preceding sigh
of content and satisfaction.

It echoes in the wind,
drifting effortlessly across the water.

Always conveying us closer
to the self we are seeking.

Roller Coaster, Carousel

Sometimes it's a roller coaster;
others, a carousel.

At times I hear a blazing guitar
wailing out a randy rock 'n' roll tune,
at others, it sings softly
a love song, nestled in
the subtleties and intimacies
of pillow talk.

I take the deep swerves
and sharp curves with little caution;
I'm poised on the painted horse
child-like, waiting for your hand
to steady me, ready me
for the ride.

Sometimes I tremble with fear,
thrash in pain; while at others,
I'm bouncing into grace,
wondering at the abundance
of affection in this beautiful world.

Through it all
you remain true.

God On Our Block

"Is that God?" you ask,
your green eyes glowing
wide open with query.

"Yes," I whisper, "that is God."

We are gazing in amazement
at a 30-foot tall Agave
next door.

"That *is* God." You repeat.

"Once it flowers, it dies." My voice
matter-of-fact, my hand trembling,
thinking about the give and take
of life and death,
all things finite.

The spike, reaching for the sky,
not yet come into full array.
Its grayish, blue-green blades
unfolding their opulence,
only a few yielding to brown.

The plant still has some time,
life left. It has grown, flourished
more than a decade, making
ready for this moment
when it dies for beauty.

Continued

We admire it,
watching a tiny humming bird
perch at its peak.

I contemplate the approaching swan song
when the spike bursts into a blossom
to glisten white in summer sun.

Like my heart opening
to your love.

Unfaded Love
for M.G.

Once, when I was young, I had lovers a plenty,
adventures galore.

The passing of years has muted the lights,
blurred names and faded faces.

But you stay in unclouded vision,
your song as strong as the first night
I found you on stage
when magic seemed to surround you.

Your music moved through my veins
like ambrosia from the gods,
compelling me to dance and sway
as you played guitar and sang,

Catching me in a web of your sparkling eyes.

I recall the touch of your lips,
the cradle of your arms,
your head resting on my breasts,
an inexplicable connection
as our souls danced above bodies entwined
in passion and eager exploration.

Continued

In those experimental days of searching,
breaking with tradition,
encounters could be casual, nonchalant
with few regrets and many fond recollections.

But you are the exception,
standing out like a star, brilliant,
ablaze in the heavens;
a memory that does not recede,
but remains as clear as
a bright wood fire, burning
on a chill autumn night.

Red Moon on the Water

Water always reminds me of you.

Black velvet nights
alive under a red moon,
sending its shine
in radiant ripples
across the water.

Like the words of your song
along my bone,
reaching into a remote
moan and whine of melancholy.

The night smells of our
musky secrets
while the air is southern comfort
sliding down my throat
in echoes of you.

I recall us entangled in hay
after Thanksgiving dinner,
looking up to find the mare
staring at us, smiling.

We were wet from walking
in the creek where
the cicada chirpings hid
in our pockets. We carried
them home, unaware.

Continued

We found seclusion in the barn
where crisp sun beams danced
across your nakedness
and the whispering wind
licked me clean.

In the tangle of memory
and rivers, I watch for you
in the moonlight, listening
for the final verse of your song.

Longing to return
to any of the moments
where our magic
held all the word at bay,
and we lost ourselves to love.

Water always reminds me of you.

Whether creek or river,
waterfall or pond. The ocean
became our home,
where we descended
to the deep blue to swim
with our beloved dolphins.

Only you decided to stay.

And I am left
to live out my days
crouching at water's edge,
remembering.

Kisses

Kisses, he said, write about kisses.

The flutter of light
butterfly kisses
alight on my eye lids,
waking me from dreams in colors.

Then I remember
our first kiss,
sneaking up on us,
a sleek black cat
on an autumn night
under a full yellow moon.

Who can resist kissing
under a full yellow moon?

It snuck up on us and
knocked us to the ground
where the earth opened,
gulping us deep down
into the cauldron
of crackling desire.

The second one came
in rapid succession,
despite an avowal of restraint.

You, splitting me wide open,
savoring the recognition.

Continued

Here the soul mate
the twin, the end
of the search.

But then, the sky began to cry
as we denied ourselves
the end of the journey.

The third kiss was chaste, guarded,
making no mistakes, taking no liberties,
risking no bold moves.

We were out to prove we could
come that close,
without combustion.

We succeeded, but not without
consequence.

The thwarted explosion
crept inside and hid out;
the imploding sparks and fiery fumes
burnt a hole in my heart
where hope slowly leaked out
murky puddles
on the ground.

After that, we kissed
with the ease of cousins,
the trust of siblings lost at sea,
orphans of the night, searching
for a guiding star
looking North.

Gently, our lips touched,
devoid of earlier longings.

Continued

A quick thing, complete into itself;
no prophecy,
no pronouncement.
Nothing to be restrained.

A statement of how far
we had come from
under the yellow moon.

A seal of our avowal of friendship,
a prologue to the times ahead where
we would mature into our full potential,
taking the higher road
back to the beginning.

Our ride into safety and decorum
lulled me into a careless disregard,
a loose-jointed acceptance.

We learned to dance at arms length;
we spoke in code,
casting distant shadows.
We left our history dangling
from a tall oak, high on the hill.

We practiced a polite withdrawal,
dismantled the tents, packed up
and headed home
where we had promises to keep.

In this state of grace,
laced with honey sweet memory,
I lapsed into unguarded ease,
never expecting to be hit
by friendly fire.

Continued

I was unaware and unprepared
for your kiss that would rekindle
dying embers
and spark the volcanic turbulence
that once again shook the earth
from under my feet,
opening up the ground,
where I was swallowed whole,
unable to grab hold
and climb back into light.

Here in the dark I reside
awaiting the brilliance
of a big yellow moon.

Under the Yellow Moon

You come again for me,
extending your arms
to scoop me into your skin,
kissing my eyes,

While muttering love words
soft and melodic, making me remember,
melting the forgetting into puddles
around my bare feet,

Where I stand under a straw roof,
dripping in wanting,
wide open to your charm.

Here you remove my fear,
brush away the tears of laughing
just to keep from crying
and gently ease me into our familiar dance
where some old blues song
drapes us in the music,

Prolonging the time
when we will reach inside, quitting our hiding,
to undo buttons of bone that hold fast
our armor against the other,

Let everything fall
where it will.

Continued

Soon we surrender
under a pale yellow moon,
listening to sea waves lap against the sand
just outside our door.

Now we are waiting for the wind
to whisper its last good-bye
before dawn breaks
our hearts again.

Once in a Blue Moon

We're listening
to Van Morrison
on the radio,
holding hands.

Calling up old memories
that warmed us
through twelve
misspent winters.

You like the scent
of roses in my hair.

I am lost in your arms
where words give way
to the music.

All around us velvet
and colors of dark wine

We laugh because
together we are
so alive.

And the yearning
reminds us.

Love or Something Like It

Love like blood
trickles down my soul
slightly sticky
deep red glow

Love like danger
laced with fear
dances on the edge
of my heart beat
when you are near

Love like candy
sweet, dark chocolate
sitting on the end
of my tongue
savored, swallowed slowly

Love like death
strangling the air
as caring
turns to control

Love like lumps
of coal waiting
to be mined
and polished
until they shine

Continued

Love like butterflies
who migrate south
in cold
searching for the sun
escaping winter's bones

Love like a lazy day
stretching beyond
noon wine, inviting
feather pillows

Love like an eagle
flying to its
secret lake
for rejuvenation

Love like a cactus flower
abloom in the wilderness
defying the draught
denying night

Love like a rose
bleeding her fragrance
onto the ground
bound for glory
ripe in sensual pleasures

Love like a bandit
the thief in the night
stealing our breath

Love like the ocean
burying our dreams
beneath tons of watery
illusions

Continued

Love like the leaf
floating on a pond
drifting its way
home, and home again

Love like a knife wound
open and oozing
ragged edges
not a clean
sharp stab

Love like dawn
riding in on the wolf
howling down
the clouds
storming through the fields
of unsown wishes

Love like a merry band
of outlaws
taking from the rich
dividing among the poor
all things
by birthright beautiful

Love like sheep grazing
on that distant hill
making wool
wishing on a shooting star
who keeps to itself

Love like a stranger
spending the night
and dropping the rose
on a pillow

Continued

where his breath
seeps deep
into your soul

Love like the sound
of fury
sweeping across a desert
raiding the camp
where babes nestle
in mothers' arms

Love like warm honey
secreting sweet seductions
a starry-eyed wink
when the wind has had
her way with you

Love like nails
in her coffin
tapping out
amazing grace

Love like a black cat
arching her back
and signaling
the beginning
of something sinister
and thrilling

Love like our Mother Earth
accepting seeds
and sowing
in accordance
with the seasons

Continued

Love like windmills
slowly in the west
where no one
whispers the name
of a brand new waltz

Love like waves washing
onto shore
violent and worthy
restless and repentant

Love like love itself
spreading its wings
and lifting off
to soar through
a midnight sky
without lights
without intentions

Denouement

I don't pretend to comprehend this falling,
where complexities
will, in the end, unravel
until it all makes sense.

This untying resembles
the weariness of waiting,
trying, relentless and unyielding.

The rising action sped by,
sweeping us into its lusty wind
to uncharted lands and secret crevices
of concealed desires.

The conflict, predictable: light vs. dark;
the climax, shocking, slightly scary –
touching on madness.

Now we are tumbling toward conclusion,
waiting in a downpour
to watch it all unfold.

Continued

Inside this falling, tumbling,
caught in uncertainty,
shrouded in timeless vapors,
unable to augur the outcome,

I am unwilling to walk out
before the final act.

Last Waltz

We are dancing the last waltz
gripped in fear,
rigid in our reluctance
to embrace the end
of what is,
to welcome
what will be reborn.

I stepped inside the fire of you,
ignoring I am wood.

The burning brands me.

You have claimed me,
naming the unspoken secret
that simmered low
until flames leapt up high,

Threatening our sanctuary
of silence.

Continued

Now we dance in the danger
as words once uttered
hang in the air
between us
where we breathe in
our own ashes,

Uncertain, dreaming
yesterday's kisses.

Revisiting the Cards

I went again to see
the Do-dah man.
He reminded me
to play my hand.

He told me to
quit holding.

So here I lay them down:

I play the Queen,
allow the King,
discarding two Deuces.

I cover Honor
with Honor.

I finesse the Jack.

I keep the Joker wild.

Jesse's Song

for Jesse 'Guitar' Taylor

When your music
extends the metaphor
transcending time,
I lose myself
to your allure.

I let you lead me.

The journey,
at once explicit
and mysterious,
meanders
up and down
my spine.

Here in the holy
tower of song
I belong
to the moment fully
immersed in your message,
no longer needing

To seek or search.

My thirst is slaked,
hunger abated,
as I bathe

Continued

in the potent beauty
of sensuous self expression
and sacred rapture.

The melody is sweet,
the rhythm, robust.

Both linger.

My heart opens
for love;
my soul surrenders
to joy.

I have come
to the fountain.

I am healed.

The symbol, which indicates the end of each poem in the deck of 52, was adapted from the drawing entitled

"THE ACE OF ROSES"
by
Jesse Taylor.

Citations

Page iii. *Deal Me In* song quotation, author unknown. Every effort was made to identify the song writer but without success.

Page 3. *Allison's Theme* music written by Donnie Gilliland, 1963.

Page 9. "Caddie's Song for Michael" was first published in *Feeding the Crow*, edited by Susan Bright, Plain View Press, 1998, pp. 171-173.

Page 29. "Beside Still Waters" was first published in *The Austin Chapter Newsletter of the Story Circle Network*, volume four, number one, Spring 2003.
"a rose cannot bloom the whole year long" quote from song *Split and Slide* written by Butch Hancock.
"slow spell" references the song *Bluebird* written by Butch Hancock.

Page 37. "Reflections" was first published on the internet at *Ancient Circles: Masks*, May 2002. http://www.ancientcircles.comm/masks.html

Page 53. "You know you've got it if it makes you feel good" and "come on, come on, come on" quotes from song *Piece of My Heart* written by Bert Berns and Jerry Ragovy, 1967, recorded by Janis Joplin, 1968,

Page 55. "Lightning Never Takes a Long Time" song quotation, written by Al Grierson.

Page 63. "Stir Carefully Through the Days" quote from song *Memories Are Made of This* written by John R. Mann, Choral Music Company, Anderson, S. C.

Page 69. "Coming to the Bone Man" was first published in *Feeding the Crow*, edited by Susan Bright, Plain View Press, 1998, pp. 183-185.

Page 97. *I'm Confessing That I Love You* song written by Guy Lombardo, 1930.
Someone to Watch Over Me song written by George and Ira Gershwin, 1926.
Alfie song written by Burt Bacharach and Hal David, 1966.
"women do get weary" quote from song *Try a Little Tenderness* written by James Campbell, Reginald Connelly and Harry Woods, 1933.
"like a captive bird that is there at your command" quote from song *First Time Ever I Saw Your Face*, written by Ewan McColl, 1962.

Page 111. "Refrain From Yearning" was first published in *The Creative Pulse of Austin*, September 2004, p. 4.

Photo by Butch Hancock

Alyce McCullough Guynn

Biography

Alyce Guynn is a long-time Austin poet with roots in the local music community. Arriving in the mid-sixties as a news reporter for the *Austin American-Statesman*, she began her poetry performances in the seventies at local music venues, the Alamo Lounge and emmajoe's. She has a 20-year career as a state antitrust investigator, and is the mother of Mercy, Justin and Geoffrey, all of whom are now grown and remain in Austin.

Alyce McCullough Guynn

Bibliography

Books

Guynn, Alyce, et al. "blood, bones and roses," *Feeding the Crow*, edited by Susan Bright. Plain View Press, Austin, Texas, 1998.

_____. *Beyond Blue: In Memory of Champ Hood, August 16th, 1952 – November 3, 2001*. Self-published, Austin, Texas, 2001.

_____. "Angels Are Wild," p. 3; "Gifts For Margaret," p. 4; "Holy Handles," p. 6; "Hope Runs Free," p. 7; "Send No Knight to Me," p. 8; "Snake Haired Woman," p. 10; "Vincent," p. 11; "Reincarnation Rose," p. 12; "The Ways of the Mother," p. 14. *Saturday Mornings; Poetry and Prose, 2001*. The Authors, Austin, Texas, 2001.

_____. "A Shiner for Rose," *New Texas 2001*, p. 159, edited by Carolyn Poulter, et al. University of Mary Hardin-Baylor, Center for Texas Studies, Belton, Texas, 2001.

_____. "Seeking Shelter in the Cove," p. ii, *Along Life's Path: A Book of Reflections*. The Seton Cove, Austin, Texas, 2002.

_____. "Meat or Fish," p. 140. *Windhover: a Journal of Christian Literature*, volume 7. University of Mary Hardin-Baylor Press, Belton, Texas, 2002.

_____. "Lost in Pageantry" and "Lotteria Tabla," *Lotteria Verses*. High Moon Writers Circle, Austin, Texas, 2004.

Periodicals

Guynn, Alyce. "Lurching Ahead," *Equinox: A Cuprunethover Book*, no. 1, Cuprunethover, Austin, Texas, Spring Equinox, 1982.

_____. "A Turquoise and Silver Day," Solstice: A Cuprunethover Book, no. 2, Cuprunethover, Austin, Texas, Summer Solstice, 1982.

_____. "Swimming to Avalon," p. 34. *2001: a di-verse-city odyssey, an austin international poetry festival anthology*, edited by Scott Wiggerman. Austin Poets International, Austin, Texas, 2001.

_____. "Chandelier Confinement, " p. 4, *The Creative Pulse of Austin*, Austin, Texas, March 2004.

_____. "Incandescent Tears," p. 9, *Austin Chapter Newsletter of the Story Circle Network*, volume 5, no. 1, Austin, Texas, Spring 2004.

_____. "Refrain of Yearning," p. 4, *The Creative Pulse of Austin*, Austin, Texas, September 2004.

_____. "Beside Still Waters," *The Austin Chapter Newsletter of the Story Circle Network*, volume 4, number 1, Austin, Texas, Spring 2003.

Music Album Notes

Guynn, Alyce. "Pumpkin and Cinnamon on Parade," *A Night in Baton Rouge* recording by Terry Clarke, not yet released.

_____. "It's All Jazz," *Low Down and Up*, recording by Toni Price, Antone's Records, 1999.

Webpages

Guynn, Alyce. "Anniversary," *Give Sorrow Words: the Day America Changed, September 11, 2001*, Story Circle Network, September 2002. http://www.storycircle.org/sorrow/guynn.html

_____. "Reflections," *Ancient Circles: Masks*, May 2002. http://www.ancientcircles.com/masks.html

_____. "Snake Haired Woman," *Awakened Woman*, April 2002. http://www.awakenedwoman.com/medussa.htm

_____. "Snake Haired Woman," *Somswordtjewakker*, March 2005. http://somswordtjewakker.web-log.nh/archief25/02/2005

_____. "War and Peace," *Poets Against the War*, February 2003. http://www.poetsagainstthewar.org/displaypoem.asp?AuthorID=5715#453063219.

_____. "grace notes," *Champ*, Gruene Hall, October 2001. http://www.corrider.net/champ/

_____. "blue moon over texas," *Tribute to Champ Hood*, 2001. http://www.toniprice.com/champ.html

Webpages, No Longer Available

_____. "women knights of the heart-shaped table," *Dream Forge Web Mag*. http://jerry.pcisys.net/~drmforge/map175-1.htm+%22women+knights+of+the+heart-shaped+table%22&hl=en

Creative Writing Awards

- 1st Place in Poetry, PHI THETA KAPPA, Alpha Gamma Pi Chapter, *Creative Writing Contest*, December 15, 1984.
- 1st Place in Short Story, PHI THETA KAPPA, Alpha Gamma Pi Chapter, *Creative Writing Contest*, December 15, 1984.
- 1st Place in Essay, PHI THETA KAPPA, Alpha Gamma Pi Chapter, *Creative Writing Contest*, Spring 1985.
- 2nd Place in Essay, PHI THETA KAPPA, Alpha Gamma Pi Chapter, *Creative Writing Contest*, Spring 1985.
- 1st Place in Short Story, PHI THETA KAPPA, Alpha Gamma Pi Chapter, *Creative Writing Contest*, Spring 1985.

Compiled by K. P. Massey and Alyce Guynn.

Photo by Butch Hancock

Jesse Taylor

Biography

Jesse Taylor has been a professional musician for over forty years. He has toured around the planet many times over and played on more than seventy albums. He did some illustrating in his youth but dropped it to concentrate on music. About three years ago he picked it up again and currently concentrates more on art than music. Taylor resides in Austin, Texas where he has lived since 1988.

Jesse Taylor
Art Catalogue: 2002-2005

Artist's Statement, Private Collection: Conni Hancock, ink.

Belize, Private Collection: Mark Andes, colored pencils.

Bush Man, colored pencils, acrylic.

Blues Power, Private Collection: Steve Power, colored pencils.

Carrie's Aries, Private Collection: Carrie Young, colored pencils, acrylic.

Chelsea's Pisces, Private Collection: Chelsea Taylor, colored pencils.

Cornflower, Private Collection: Chelsea Taylor, acrylic.

Dracula, colored pencils.

Follicle Man, Private Collection: Tim Johnson, colored pencils.

Frankie the Junkie, Private Collection: Mandy Mercier, charcoal pencil.

Guitar Party , colored pencils, acrylic.

Houston Bird, Private Collection: Alyce Guynn, colored pencils, acrylic.

Insanity, colored pencils.

Jazz in the 21st Century, Private Collection: Kathy Taylor, colored pencils.

King Kong, Private Collection: Brad and Lynn Brobisky , colored pencils.

Leaf Fish, mixed media.

Lovers, colored pencils.

Meditation, Private Collection: Leea Mechling, colored pencils.

Mermaid, Private Collection: Nicole Taylor, colored pencils.

Nicole's Pisces, Private Collection: Nicole Taylor, colored pencils.

Phoenix Rising, , colored pencils, acrylic.

Piano Man, Private Collection: Nicole Taylor, charcoal pencil.

Playing Cards, Private Collection: Alyce Guynn, colored pencils.

Political Pig, Private Collection: Amy Manor, charcoal pencil.

Rage, Private Collection: Chelsea Taylor, colored pencils.

Renaldo & Clara (Suspicion), Private Collection: Brad and Lynn Brobiski, colored pencils.

Rooster, colored pencils.
Roses and Roosters, Private Collection: Nicole Taylor, colored pencils, acrylic.
Saved , Private Collection: Jeff Wheeler, colored pencils, acrylic.
Schizophrenia Man, Private Collection: Jim Franklin, water color.
Sigmund, Private Collection: John Northland, colored pencils.
Stella, Private Collection: Kim Stewart, colored pencils.
Sun, Private Collection: Davis McClarty, colored pencils, acrylic.
The Ace of Roses, Private Collection: Alyce Guynn, colored pencils, acrylic.
The Jockey, Private Collection: Mandy Mercier, colored pencils.
The Old Rugged Cross, colored pencils, acrylic.
The Wizard, Private Collection: Victoria, colored pencils.
Tim's Leo, Private Collection: Tim Fain, colored pencils.
Totem Pole, Private Collection: Carrie Young, colored pencils, acrylic.

Compiled by Alyce Guynn and Jesse Taylor.

Jesse Taylor

Partial Discography: 1978-2005

Jesse Taylor, *Last Night*, Tornado Alley Records, 1988.
Jesse Taylor, *Texas Tattoo*, Appaloosa, 1998.
Jesse Taylor and Tornado Alley, *Live Set on Air. Vol. 3*, KUT, 1994.
Jesse Taylor, Jack Billingsly, *Michigan/I Never Traded Diamonds*, Texas Soul, 1988.
Jesse Taylor, John Reed, *Southside Guitar*, South Congress Records, 2001.
Jesse Taylor, Terry Clarke, Michael Messer, *Rhythm Oil: The Sessions*, Minidoka Records, 1993.
Joe Ely, *Joe Ely*, MCA, 1997.
Joe Ely, *Honky Tonk Masquerade*, MCA, 1978.
Joe Ely, *Down on the Drag*, MCA, 1979.
Joe Ely, *Twisting in the Wind*, MCA, 1998.
Joe Ely, *Live Shots*, MCA, 1980.
Joe Ely, *Live at Antone's*, Rounder, 2000.
Joe Ely, *Musta Notta Gotta Lotta*, MCA, 1981.
Joe Ely, *Best of Joe Ely*, MCA, 2000.
Joe Ely, *Milkshakes and Malts*, Sun Storm Records, 1988.
Joe Ely, *Whatever Happened to Maria*, Sun Storm Records, 1989.
Joe Ely, *Texas Special*, Southcoast Records (MCA), 1981.
Stubb/Jesse Taylor/Joe Ely, *Stubb's Legendary Cookbook*, 1991.
Terry Allen, *Lubbock (On Everything)*, Fate Records, 1979.
Terry Allen, *Human Remains*, Sugar Hill, 1996.
Terry Allen, *Bloodlines*, Fate Records, 1984.
Terry Allen, *Smokin' the Dummy*, Fate Records, 1980.
Terry Clarke, *Lucky*, Appaloosa, 1998.
Terry Clarke, *Green Voodoo*, Catfish, 2001.
Michael Messer, *King Guitar*, Catfish, 1999.

Billy Joe Shaver, Kinky Friedman, *Live from Down Under*, Sphincter Records, 2002.
Marcia Ball, *Gatorhythms*, Rounder, 1989.
Butch Hancock, *No Two Alike*, Rainlight, 1995.
Butch Hancock, *Own and Own*, Rainlight, 1989.
Butch Hancock, *Eats Away the Night*, Sugar Hill, 1995.
Jimmie Dale Gilmore, *After a While*, Elektra Nonesuch, 1992.
Ponty Bone, *My, My Look At This*, Amazing Records, 1988.
Ponty Bone, *Dig Us On The Road Somewhere*, Real World Records, 1995.
Kimmie Rhodes, *Jackalopes, Moons and Angels*, Jackalopes Records, 1998.
Kimmie Rhodes, *West Texas Heaven*, Sunbird Records, 1996.
Kimmie Rhodes, *Angels Get the Blues*, Heartland Records, 1989.
Maines Brothers, *Panhandle Dancer*, Texas Soul, 1982.
Maines Brothers, *Rt. 1 Acuff, Texas Soul, 1980.*
Supernatural Family Band , *Texas Inlaws*, 1978.
Supernatural Family Band, *Live at the Little Bear*, 1978.
Supernatural Family Band, *Real George*, Akashic Recordings, 1978.
Tommy Hancock, *Lubbock Lights*, Akashic Recordings, 1986.
The Keepers, *Looking for a Sign*, Lizard Discs, 1995.
The Keepers, *Every Dog Is A Star*, Dog Disc Music, 1997.
Brad Brobisky, *Painted Pony*, Lizard Disc, 1999.
Benny Rye, *Benny Rye*, South Congress Records, 2001.
Rachel Lane, featuring Jesse 'Guitar' Taylor, *Rachel Lane and the Chain Smokin' Poor Boys.*
Jimmy LaFave, Tomato (not released).
Mary Welch, *Visions of You*, South Congress Records, 2001.
Texas Bel-Airs, *The Texas Bel Airs*, 1999.
Don McCallister, *Born in a Hurricane*, Appaloosa, 2001.
Don Yarborough, *Heaven Help Us*, Folk Era, 2004.
Eric Blakely, *Growing Into My Father's Clothes*, Folk Reel , 1993.
Eric Blakely, *Payne Anthology*, Folk Reel.
Teye, *El Gitano Punky*, 1988.
Michael Lebraton, *Absotively Posolutely*, 1995.
Janine Wilson, *The Blue Album*, Biscuit Boy, 2000.

Charles Terry, *Honkin'*, Texas Soul, 1980.

Steve Power and Jesse Taylor, *Somewhere in Texas and Flying My Way Home*, 2004.

Cathouse Blues, *Cold Jealous Fingers*, 1993.

HooDoo Cats, *HooDoo Time*, Bjam Records, 1994.

Jimmy Hofer, *Austin…Oder So*, Sound Service, 1994.

Jimmy Hofer, *Born in Bern*, Sound Service, 1995.

Various Artists, *Get Weaving, Vol. 3*, Weaving Records, 1996.

Various Artists, *A Taste of Sugar Hill's Texas Singer-Songwriters*, Sugar Hill.

Various Artists, *Blues Road Trip: City to City*.

Various Artists, *Not Fade Away (Remembering Buddy Holly)*.

Various Artists, *Across the Great Divide: The Songs of Jo Carol Pierce*, DejaDisc, 1992.

Various Artists, *Big Guitars from Texas "That's Cool That's Trash,"* 1986.

Various Artists, *More Big Guitars From Texas "That's Cool That's Trash,"* 1986.

Various Artists, *Best of Mountain Stage Live*, Vol. 2, 1991.

Various Artists, *Country Routes*, MCA, 1978.

Various Artists, *Blue Devil Sampler*, Bedrock Records, 1990.

Various Artists, *Blues Guitar Box*, 1990.

Various Artists, *Welcome to Transatlantic Country*, Transatlantic, 1996.

Various Artists, *Roots Music: An American Journey*.

Song written by Jesse Taylor, recorded by:

Duke LaRue and the Blue Jukes, *One O'Clock in the Morning*, "One A.M. Blues," Duke Records, 1992.

Compiled by Alyce Guynn and Jesse Taylor.

PEARSON PUBLISHING COMPANY
CORPUS CHRISTI, TEXAS

For a complete list and description of our publications and to order books please go to our website:

www.PearsonPub.US

Deal Me In
    By Alyce Guynn with illustrations by
    Jesse Taylor $23.95

My Metrical Metamorphosis
    By author and illustrator Nicole Niewoehner
    $23.95

Angels Are In Charge
    By Frances Cotten Woodard
    $23.95

The Sacred Gifts
    By Katherine Jagoe Massey. $19.95

To mail in orders send (1) a list of titles with number of copies of each title, (2) check or money order including total retail price for all books, plus (3) $3.00 for shipping per book, and (4) your name and mailing address printed clearly, to:

Pearson Publishing Company
711 N. Carancahua, Suite 119
Corpus Christi, Texas 78475

Or go to bn.com or amazon.com to purchase.

To purchase art or recordings by Jesse Taylor go to the Pearson Publishing Company webpage for a link to Taylor's webpages: www.PearsonPub.US

www.ingramcontent.com/pod-product-compliance
Lightning Source LLC
Chambersburg PA
CBHW071607170426
43196CB00034B/2182